Sports Records

Football Records

by Anthony K. Hewson

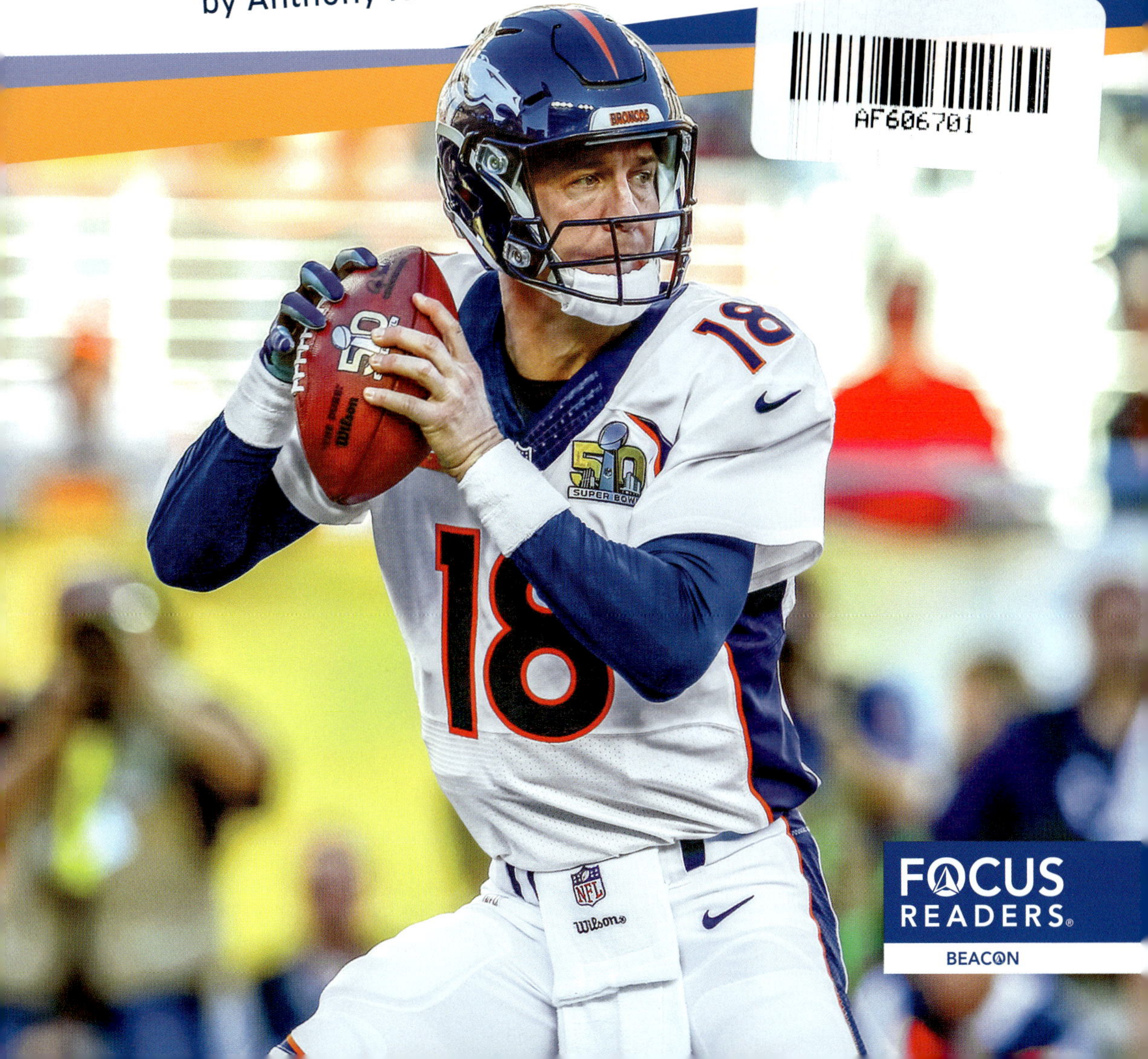

FOCUS READERS

BEACON

www.focusreaders.com

Focus Readers is distributed by North Star Editions:
sales@northstareditions.com | 888-417-0195

Produced for Focus Readers by Red Line Editorial.

Photographs ©: Ben Liebenberg/AP Images, cover, 1; Jack Dempsey/AP Images, 4; Rick Osentoski/AP Images, 7; Vernon Biever/AP Images, 8; Allen Kee/AP Images, 11; William P. Straeter/AP Images, 13; Wilfredo Lee/AP Images, 14; Peter Read Miller/AP Images, 17; Al Messerschmidt/AP Images, 19, 29; Gregory Payan/AP Images, 20; Bill Haber/AP Images, 23; Tony Tomsic/AP Images, 25; Four Seams Images/AP Images, 26–27

Library of Congress Cataloging-in-Publication Data
Names: Hewson, Anthony K., author.
Title: Football records / by Anthony K. Hewson.
Description: Lake Elmo : Focus Readers, [2021] | Series: Sports records | Includes index. | Audience: Grades 4-6
Identifiers: LCCN 2020003744 (print) | LCCN 2020003745 (ebook) | ISBN 9781644933619 (Hardcover) | ISBN 9781644934371 (Paperback) | ISBN 9781644935132 (eBook) | ISBN 9781644935897 (PDF)
Subjects: LCSH: Football--Records--United States--Juvenile literature. | Sports records--United States.
Classification: LCC GV955 .H49 2021 (print) | LCC GV955 (ebook) | DDC 796.33202/02--dc23
LC record available at https://lccn.loc.gov/2020003744
LC ebook record available at https://lccn.loc.gov/2020003745

Printed in the United States of America
Mankato, MN
122022

About the Author

Anthony K. Hewson is a freelance writer, originally from San Diego, now living in the Bay Area with his wife and their two dogs.

Table of Contents

Riddell
18
NFL
18
BRONCOS
18

Chapter 1

Peyton's Passes

Peyton Manning dropped back to pass. He looked to his right. Julius Thomas was open. Manning heaved a deep ball to the receiver. It landed perfectly in Thomas's hands. Touchdown!

Peyton Manning played for the Indianapolis Colts before moving to the Denver Broncos.

It was an easy throw for the quarterback to make. But this throw was Manning's 51st touchdown pass of 2013. That broke the record for touchdown passes in a National Football League (NFL) season. Manning finished the season with 55.

Julius Thomas left the record-breaking football on the field after celebrating. Fortunately, a teammate picked up the ball and gave it to Manning.

Peyton Manning was the first quarterback to win the Super Bowl on multiple teams.

Chapter 2

Tremendous Teams

The NFL has had many great teams. But the 1972 Miami Dolphins were the first to be perfect. The Dolphins won all 14 games in the regular season.

In 1972, Dolphins Mercury Morris (22) and Larry Csonka were the first duo to have more than 1,000 rushing yards.

Then they won all three of their **playoff** games. Miami finished with a perfect record of 17–0.

The NFL later moved to a longer 16-game schedule. The 2007 New England Patriots were the first team to win all 16 games. They won two playoff games to go 18–0. But the Patriots lost in the Super Bowl.

Baltimore's Shutouts

The 2000 Baltimore Ravens had an amazing **defense**. They helped the Ravens win the Super Bowl.

Ravens linebacker Ray Lewis (52) tackles a New York Giants player during Super Bowl XXXV.

The team was led by Ray Lewis and Rod Woodson. The Ravens allowed a record-low 165 points during the season. They also **shut out** four teams.

Unstoppable Sooners

Perfect seasons are more common in college football than in the NFL. And the University of Oklahoma Sooners had three perfect seasons in a row. From 1954 to 1956, the Sooners were unbeatable. The team won 47 consecutive games during

The University of Oklahoma began its football program in 1895. The team won its first national championship that year.

Running back Tommy McDonald (left) never lost a game during his time with the Sooners.

that stretch. In the 60 years that followed, no team even won 40 in a row.

C-USA

Chapter 3

Super Seasons

Bailey Zappe played quarterback for Western Kentucky University. He came into the 2021 Boca Raton Bowl with 56 touchdown passes. The college football record for most in a season was 60.

Bailey Zappe threw for 422 yards in the 2021 Boca Raton Bowl.

Zappe was on fire. He threw six touchdown passes in the Boca Raton Bowl. That set a new record. Zappe had 62 touchdown passes in a single season. He also helped his team win the game. Western Kentucky cruised to a 59–38 victory.

Zappe set another record in 2021. He threw for 5,967 yards. That was the most ever in a single season.

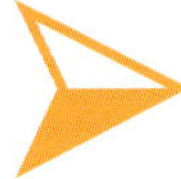

Eric Dickerson was selected for the Pro Bowl six times.

What a Rush

In 1984, Eric Dickerson set the NFL's single-season **rushing** record. He ran for 2,105 yards that year.

It has proven to be a hard record to break. Adrian Peterson came close in 2012. He missed by just nine yards.

Record-Breaking Rookie

Randy Moss burst onto the NFL scene in 1998. The wide receiver set a **rookie** record with

Moss was a touchdown machine. He led the NFL in touchdowns in five different seasons.

Randy Moss finished his NFL career with 157 touchdowns.

17 touchdowns. Nine years later, he was still going strong. Moss caught 23 touchdowns in 2007. That was a record for any receiver.

PATRIOTS
PATRIOTS
12
NFL

Chapter 4

Incredible Careers

The Super Bowl is the biggest game in football. And no player has won more Super Bowls than Tom Brady. The star quarterback won the game seven times in his **career**.

Tom Brady led the New England Patriots to an overtime victory in Super Bowl LI.

One of Brady's greatest Super Bowl moments came in 2017. The Patriots were down by 25 points in the third quarter. But Brady led his team to a victory. It was the biggest **comeback** in Super Bowl history.

Rice Can Catch

Jerry Rice played 20 NFL seasons, and he was great in all of them. Rice holds the records for most catches and most receiving yards. But one record stands above them all. Rice scored 208 touchdowns

Jerry Rice played 16 seasons with the San Francisco 49ers.

during his career. No **active** players are anywhere close to breaking Rice's record.

Run, Emmitt, Run

When it comes to running, no one gained more yards than Emmitt Smith. The running back played 15 seasons in the NFL. He ran for more than 1,000 yards in 11 of them. By the end of his career, Smith had run for 18,355 yards.

Kicker Morten Andersen played the most games of any NFL player. From 1982 to 2007, he played in 382 games.

In 1990, Emmitt Smith was a first-round draft pick for the Dallas Cowboys.

The Iron Man

Brett Favre **started** his first NFL game in Week 4 of the 1992 season. He didn't miss another game until 2010. Favre started 297 games in a row at quarterback. That is the most of any quarterback in history. During Favre's streak, 238 different quarterbacks started an NFL game.

Favre did more than just start games. He was one of the greatest quarterbacks of all time. In the 1996 season, he led the Green Bay Packers to a Super Bowl win.

Brett Favre played for the Green Bay Packers for 16 seasons.

Wilson
PACKERS

FOCUS ON

Football Records

Write your answers on a separate piece of paper.

1. Write a letter to a friend summarizing Tom Brady's career.
2. Which football record in this book do you think is the most impressive? Why?
3. Who holds the record for most career receiving yards?
   - A. Randy Moss
   - B. Jerry Rice
   - C. Peyton Manning
4. Why is Brett Favre's record unlikely to be broken?
   - A. Football is a tough sport, and injuries are common.
   - B. Teams don't play as many games as they used to.
   - C. Quarterbacks aren't allowed to play a full season anymore.

5. What does **heaved** mean in this book?

*Manning **heaved** a deep ball to the receiver. It landed perfectly in Thomas's hands.*

A. ran
B. threw
C. tackled

6. What does **consecutive** mean in this book?

*The team won 47 **consecutive** games during that stretch. In the 60 years that followed, no team even won 40 in a row.*

A. like a machine
B. perfect
C. all in a row

Answer key on page 32.

Glossary

active
Still playing in a league.

career
The total amount of time that an athlete plays his or her sport.

comeback
A situation where a team is losing but ends up winning the game.

defense
The group of players who try to stop the other team from scoring.

playoff
A set of games played after the regular season to decide which team will be the champion.

rookie
A professional athlete in his or her first year.

rushing
Running with the ball in a football game.

shut out
Stopped the other team from scoring any points in a game.

started
Began a game on the field.

To Learn More

BOOKS

Cooper, Robert. *Great Moments in NFL History*. Minneapolis: Abdo Publishing, 2020.

Hetrick, Hans. *Football's Record Breakers*. North Mankato, MN: Capstone Press, 2017.

Mason, Tyler. *Football Trivia*. Minneapolis: Abdo Publishing, 2016.

NOTE TO EDUCATORS

Visit **www.focusreaders.com** to find lesson plans, activities, links, and other resources related to this title.

Index

Answer Key: 1. Answers will vary; **2.** Answers will vary; **3.** B; **4.** A; **5.** B; **6.** C